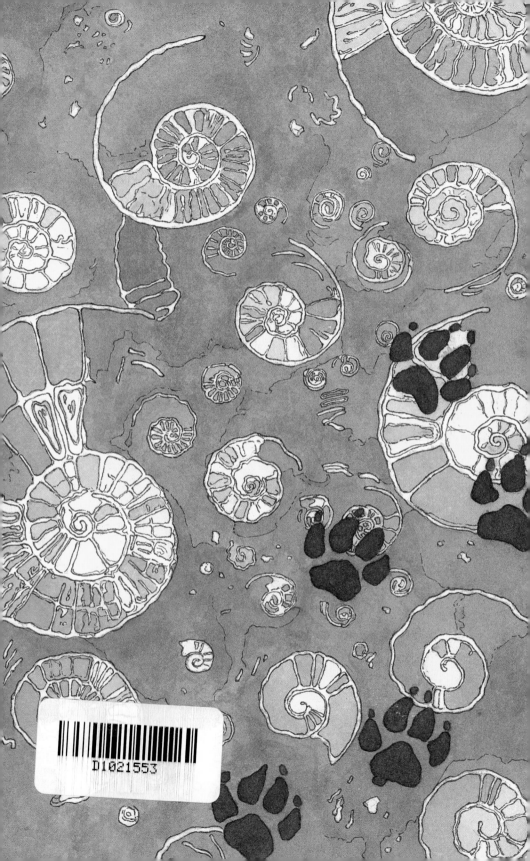

By Shirley Raye Redmond

Illustrated by Simon Sullivan

The Dog That Dug for Dinosaurs

A TRUE STORY

Aladdin

New York   London   Toronto   Sydney

First Aladdin Paperbacks edition July 2004
Text copyright © 2004 by Shirley Raye Redmond
Illustrations copyright © 2004 by Simon Sullivan

ALADDIN PAPERBACKS
An imprint of Simon & Schuster Children's Publishing Division
1230 Avenue of the Americas, New York, NY 10020

Book design by Debra Sfetsios
The text of this book was set in Century Old Style.
Printed in the United States of America
6 8 10 9 7

Library of Congress Cataloging-in-Publication Data

Redmond, Shirley-Raye.
The dog that dug for dinosaurs / by Shirley Raye Redmond ; illustrated by Simon Sullivan.—
1st Aladdin Paperbacks ed.
p. cm. — (Ready-to-read)
Summary: Relates the true story of a dog who helped his owner, twelve-year-old Mary Ann
Anning, to find dinosaur bones in Lyme Regis, England, including an ichthyosaurus,
a plesiosaur, and the first pterodactyl.
ISBN 978-0-689-85708-9 (pbk.) — ISBN 978-0-689-85709-6 (hc)
0910 LAK
1. Dinosaurs—Juvenile literature. 2. Tray (Dog)—Juvenile literature. 3. Dogs—England—
Lyme Regis—Biography—Juvenile literature. [1. Dinosaurs. 2. Tray (Dog) 3. Dogs.] I. Sullivan,
Simon, ill. II. Title. III. Series.
QE861.5.R43 2004
567.9—dc22
2003016821

A LONG, LONG TIME AGO, there was a little dog named Tray. He was black-and-white all over. He had friendly brown eyes and a very wiggily tail. Tray lived in England. Tray was a real dog, and this is an honestly true story about him.

Tray loved two things most
in the whole world. First, he loved
Mary Ann Anning. She was twelve years
old and lived with her family in a small
cottage near the beach in Lyme Regis.
Secondly, Tray loved going with Mary
Ann to dig for fossils.

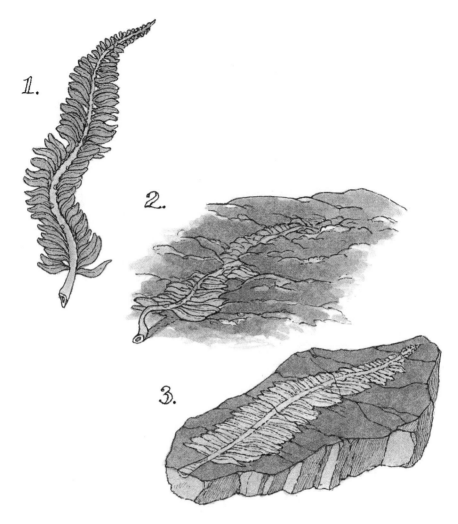

1.

2.

3.

So, what are fossils anyway? They are the remains of animals and plants that died a long time ago. When a leaf or bone gets pressed between layers of sea mud, it leaves an imprint. After many, many years, the mud hardens to rock.

Tray and Mary Ann knew that they
would find the very best fossils high
up on the cliffs around the beach. They
climbed up there every day.

Tray sniffed the rocks.

Sniff, sniff.

He pawed the dirt.

Scratch, scratch.

Mary Ann used a small hammer and
chisel.

Tap, tap, tap.

With these tools, Mary Ann carefully cut fossils out of the cliff, just as her father had shown her. Tray watched as she placed the fossils in her basket. Most of them looked like seashells. Mary Ann and Tray sold them as souvenirs to the tourists that came by stagecoach to swim at the beach near their home.

One day Tray and Mary Ann
discovered some very large bones
sticking out of the rocks. They were *huge*!

Tray growled and tried to dig the
bones out.

Mary Ann used her hands to brush
away the loose dirt.

"Tray, we've discovered a monster!"
she declared.

The bones were much too big for Tray
and Mary Ann to remove by themselves.

"I'll go for help," Mary Ann said. "You
stay here, Tray."

Tray barked loudly and sat down in
front of the bones. He was a very good
guard dog.

Mary Ann ran all the way back to town and asked some grown-ups to help her. "Tray and I have found something really special in the cliff," she told them. "Just wait and see!"

When the men saw the giant rib bones in the side of the cliff, they were amazed. "What a beast!" they cried.

"Look at those sharp teeth!"

"Is it a crocodile?" one man asked.

"Or a stubby whale?"

"We don't know what it is," Mary Ann admitted. "But we know it's something special, don't we, Tray?"

Tray yipped and wagged his tail.

A rich man who lived nearby heard about the sea monster. He hurried to see it for himself.

"I'll buy it!" he cried. "I will give it to the British Museum in London."

"Do you know what it is?" Mary Ann asked.

"It is called an ichthyosaur," the man told her.

ICK-thee-ah-soar

"That means 'fish lizard,'" he explained. "It's like a dinosaur with fins."

The amazing news spread about the gigantic fish lizard and the dog and little girl who had found it.

Soon many strangers came to Lyme Regis where Mary Ann and Tray lived. They all wanted to hunt for fossils too. The men wore tall top hats. The women wore frilly bonnets. They carried pretty little umbrellas called parasols.

Mary Ann shook her head and smiled. She rubbed Tray's soft ears. They watched the strangers together.

"They don't have the right tools," Mary Ann whispered. "They are wearing the wrong kinds of shoes. Aren't they silly, Tray?"

Tray yipped and chased his tail.

Curious scientists visited Lyme Regis too. One man came from the university in Oxford. His name was William Buckland. He went to the old carpenter's shop where Mary Ann and Tray sold their fossils.

"Can you show me where you found your ichthyosaur, young lady?" he asked politely. "Do you think you could find the exact spot again?"

"Tray can find it," Mary Ann boasted.

Together Mary Ann and Mr. Buckland
followed the little dog across the beach
and up to the cliffs.

Tray sniffed the rocks.

Sniff, sniff.

He pawed the dirt.

Scratch, scratch.

Suddenly he yipped. Then he sat down. Mary Ann pointed. It was the exact place where she had discovered the strange fish lizard!

"What an intelligent dog!" Mr. Buckland declared.

Tray wagged his tail.

Tray and Mary Ann continued to dig
for fossils. They were very careful. Mary
Ann watched for falling rocks, like her
dad told her. Tray looked out for storms
and high tides. Then one day they
discovered another giant creature.

"Look, Tray!" Mary Ann cried.

"Is it a sea dragon?"

Tray sniffed the skeleton and snapped at it with his teeth. The creature had a long, long neck. Its backbone was like a humped turtle shell. Instead of feet and legs, it had four large paddles.

But it wasn't a sea dragon.

Mr. Buckland called it a plesiosaur.

PLEE-zee-uh-sor

One day, Tray and Mary Ann found a fossil that no one in England had every found before. This one had huge bony wings like a bat and a long sharp jaw.

Tray growled.

"It looks like a gigantic flying lizard!" Mary Ann declared.

The scientists thought so too, and that's why they named it a pterodactyl.

TAIR–ah–DACK–til

That means "lizard with wings."

Over the years, Tray, Mary Ann, and
Mr. Buckland became good friends.
   They showed him where to find the
best fossils in Lyme Regis.

Mr. Buckland brought books about
dinosaurs for Mary Ann. He brought
beef bones for Tray. Mary Ann, with Tray
on her lap, studied her books every day.

When Tray's whiskers turned gray and Mary Ann was all grown up, they still collected fossils and sold them in the old carpenter's shop. There were boxes and baskets filled with fossils on the floor and on the shelves. Some of the fossil creatures were so big they couldn't fit through the door!

Sometimes children and tourists stopped in to buy fossils of ancient sand dollars or tiny fish and curly shells. Many scientists came to the shop to buy fossils too. They brought carts and wagons to haul away the really large ones.

Once a German king stopped at the shop to buy fossils for his collection and so did the Duke of Buckingham.

Tray and Mary Ann Anning became very famous. Today, if you go to the Natural History Museum in London, you can see the large fossils they discovered together.

You can also see a famous painting of Mary Ann holding her fossil basket, and Tray, the dog that dug for dinosaurs.